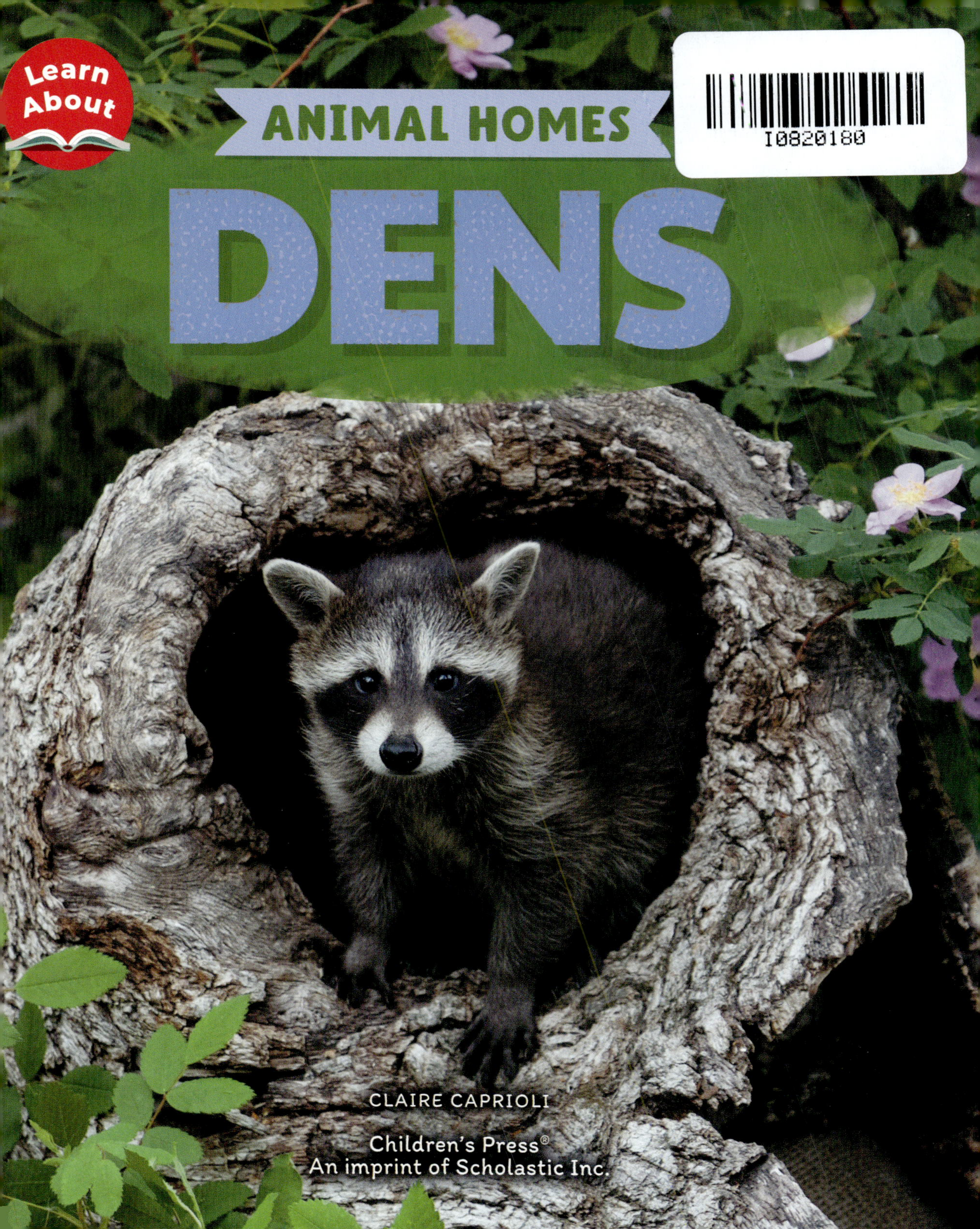

ANIMAL HOMES

DENS

CLAIRE CAPRIOLI

Children's Press®
An imprint of Scholastic Inc.

A special thank-you to the Cincinnati Zoo & Botanical Garden for their expert consultation.

Library of Congress Cataloging-in-Publication Data available

ISBN 978-1-5461-7724-1 (library binding) | ISBN 978-1-5461-7725-8 (paperback)

10 9 8 7 6 5 4 3 2 1 26 27 28 29 30

Printed in China 62

First edition, 2026

Book design by Kay Petronio

Photos ©: cover, 1: Dee Carpenter Photography/Getty Images; 6-7 grass and throughout: SpicyTruffel/Getty Images; 8-9: Photo by James Keith/Getty Images; 10: KenCanning/Getty Images; 11 inset: Paul Souders/Getty Images; 13 inset: Paul Souders/Getty Images; 14: Leonid Korchenko/Getty Images; 15 main: Jack Glisson/Alamy Images; 15 inset: Leonid Korchenko/Getty Images; 16-17: Juergen Christine Sohns/imageBROKER/Shutterstock; 17 top inset: Leonid Korchenko/Getty Images; 18: SteveByland/Getty Images; 19 main: yhelfman/Getty Images; 20-21: Jeff Lepore/Alamy Images; 22: FRANKHILDEBRAND/Getty Images; 23 main: Juniors Bildarchiv GmbH/Alamy Images; 24-25: lavin photography/Getty Images; 26: Gail Shotlander/Getty Images; 28: Ernst Mutchnick/Alamy Images; 29: Design Pics/Getty Images; 30: Natural History Archive/Alamy Images.

All other photos © Shutterstock.

CONTENTS

INTRODUCTION

SNUG DENS

A den is a shelter for wild animals. It is a place where animals feel cozy and safe. Animal dens can be found in many places. A den can be inside a cave or a pile of rocks. It can be inside a hollow log or in a hole in a tree. It can even be in the ground. Let's learn about how different animals find and use dens!

Raccoons often use a hole in a tree as a den.

Chapter 1

BOBCATS

FACT FILE

ANIMAL GROUP: Mammal

DIET: Carnivore

HABITATS: Deserts, forests, mountains, swamps

A bobcat peeks out of its rocky den.

Bobcats are bigger than most pet cats. And they like to live alone! Bobcats will make a den where they are safe and cool. This can be a hollow log or a rocky area. They will also make a den in a low branch on a tree. Bobcats usually have spotted fur. Their coloring helps them camouflage in nature. It blends in with the rocks, trees, and ground around them.

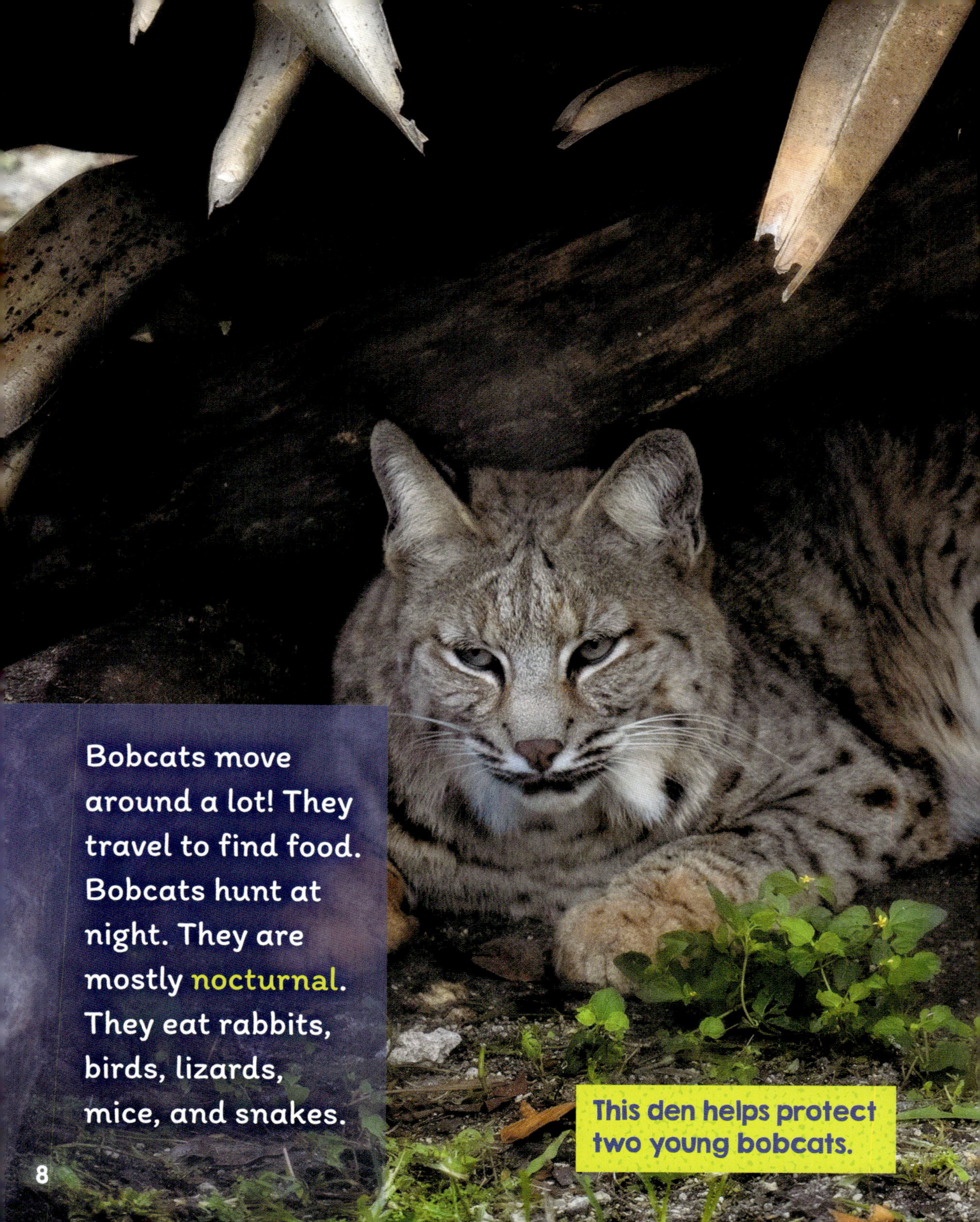

Bobcats move around a lot! They travel to find food. Bobcats hunt at night. They are mostly nocturnal. They eat rabbits, birds, lizards, mice, and snakes.

This den helps protect two young bobcats.

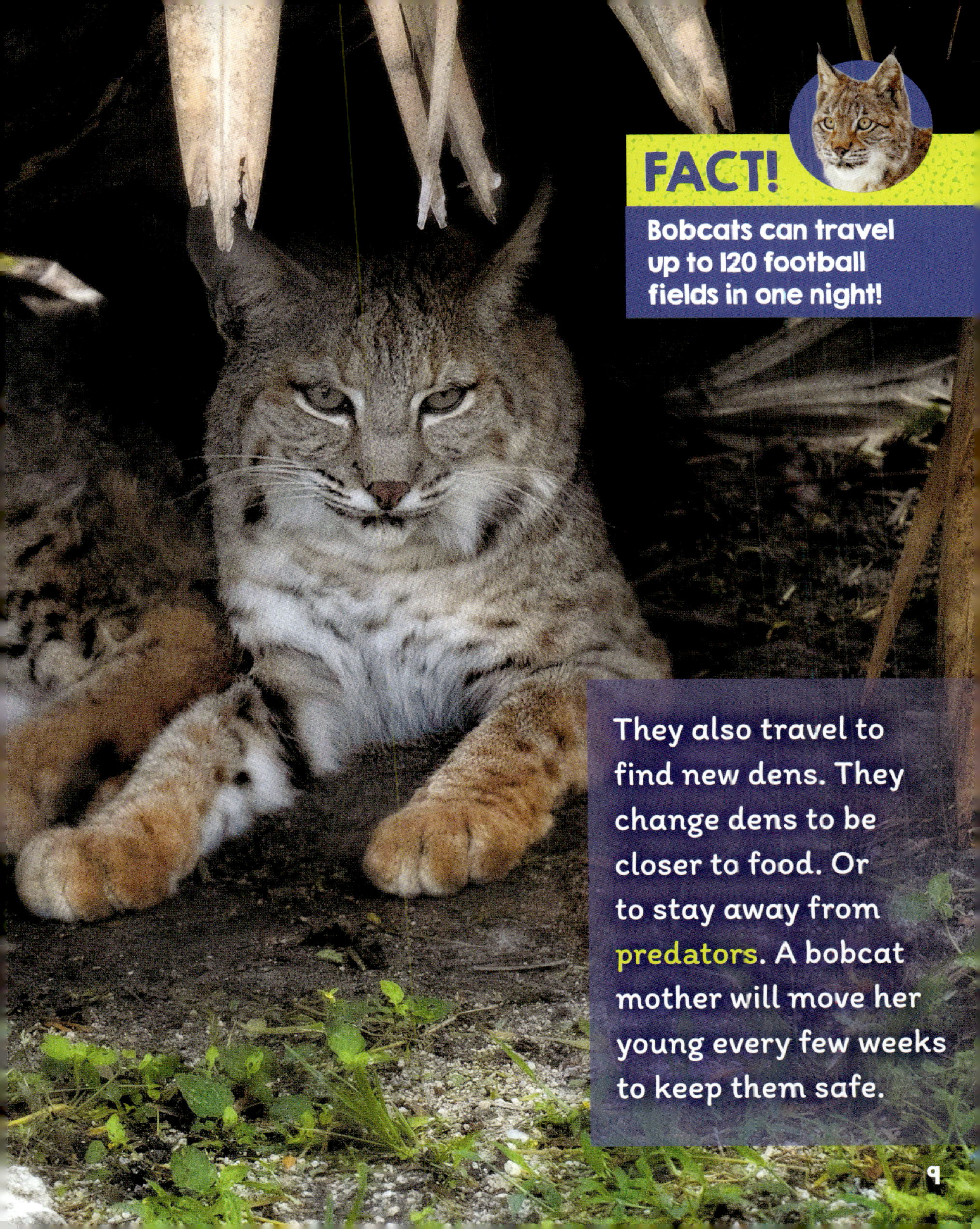

FACT!

Bobcats can travel up to 120 football fields in one night!

They also travel to find new dens. They change dens to be closer to food. Or to stay away from predators. A bobcat mother will move her young every few weeks to keep them safe.

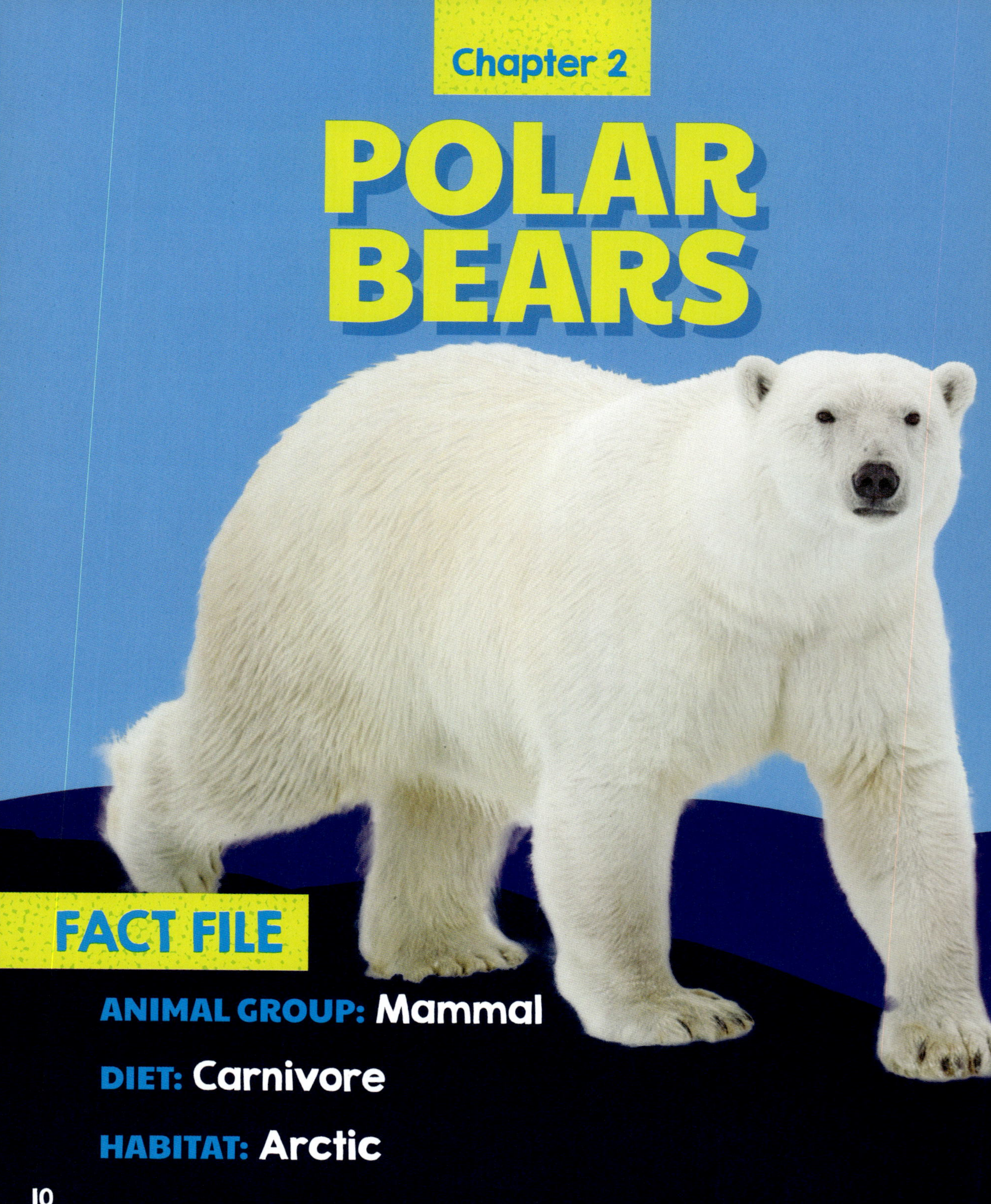

Chapter 2

POLAR BEARS

FACT FILE

ANIMAL GROUP: Mammal

DIET: Carnivore

HABITAT: Arctic

FACT!

A polar bear's outer layer of fur isn't white! The fur is made of clear hollow tubes that look white.

Polar bears use their sharp claws to dig dens in the snow and ice.

Brrrrr! Polar bears have thick, warm coats. Their fur protects them from the cold Arctic temperatures. They often sleep curled up on the ice and snow. Male polar bears only use dens if there is very harsh weather. They may create a den in the snow to block the wind. They do not need the den once the harsh weather passes.

Female polar bears have an important reason to make a den. They need to keep their babies safe and warm! Mothers give birth inside the den. The newborn babies are small and pink.

FACT!

Young polar bears are called cubs. They only weigh 1 pound (0.5 kg) at birth! That is as much as a box of pasta.

The mother does not eat for months while she stays with her babies. They leave the den together in spring. By then, the cubs are stronger and they have enough fur to protect them from the cold.

A mom and her cub play outside the entrance to their den.

Chapter 3

OPOSSUMS

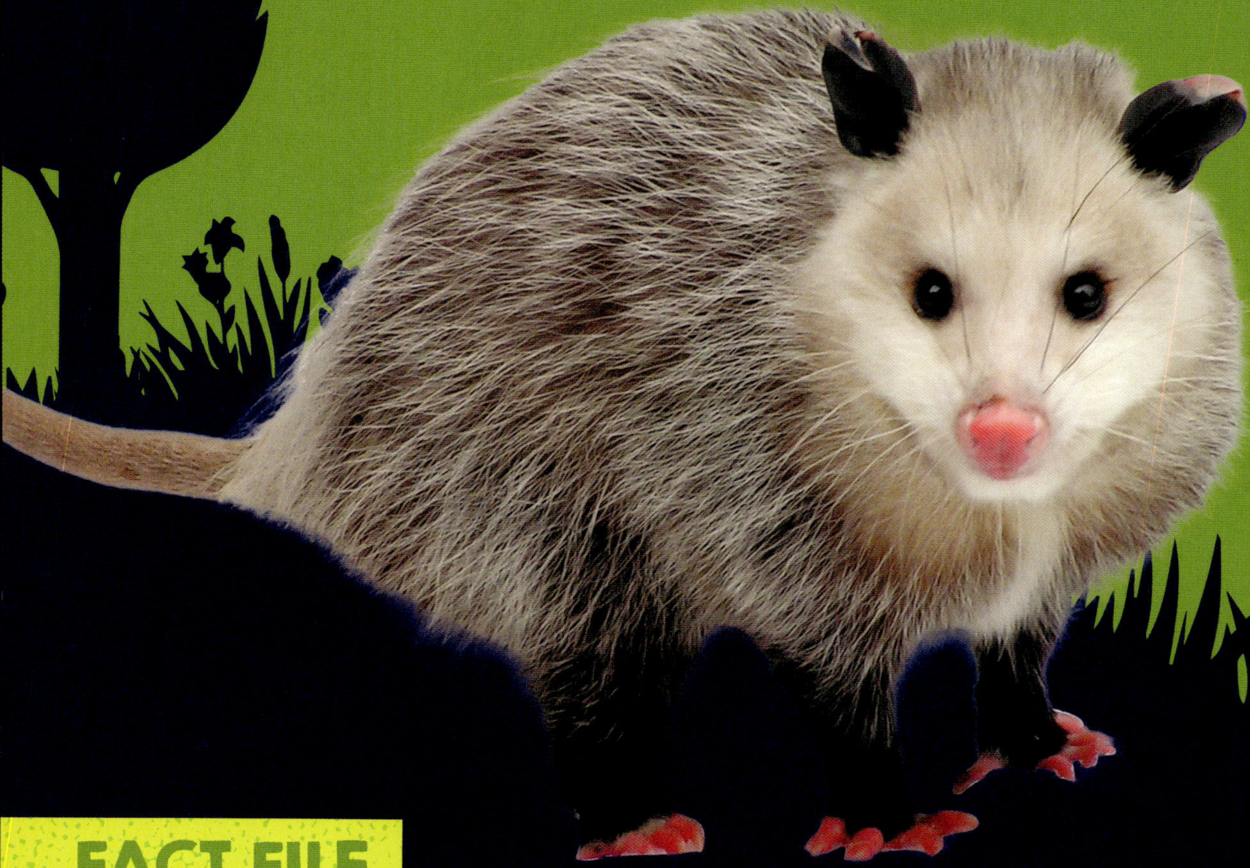

FACT FILE

ANIMAL GROUP: Mammal

DIET: Omnivore

HABITATS: Backyards, near ponds and streams, swamps, woodlands

FACT!

Opossums will also make dens under decks and sheds.

Opossum babies are called joeys.

Opossums look like large rats, but they are not! Opossums are the only marsupials found in North America. A marsupial is an animal with a pouch. A mother opossum will keep her babies safe inside her pouch for two months. The babies stay in the pouch while the mother stays in a den. Opossums make dens in trees, brush piles, and inside hollow logs. They may also use homes that other animals left as dens.

Opossums like to move around to different dens. But they do not travel very far. They stay in their dens during the day. At night they look for food. Opossums like to make their dens cozy. They use their tail to carry leaves and grass to their den. The leaves and grass make the den soft.

FACT!

When an opossum is threatened, it "plays dead." It stays like this until the predator goes away.

These opossums made a den inside a hole in a tree.

Chapter 4

RATTLESNAKES

FACT FILE

ANIMAL GROUP: Reptile

DIET: Carnivore

HABITATS: Deserts, forests, grasslands, mountains, public spaces, rocky areas, swamps

FACT!

What's that rattling sound? Rattlesnakes are named for their tail. The rattling sound is a warning to other animals to stay away!

Some rattlesnakes makes dens in empty animal burrows.

Like other reptiles, rattlesnakes are cold-blooded. They do not like very hot or very cold weather. In the hot months they live alone. They find dens that are cool. Under shrubs and rocks are good spots to find shade from the sun. They are also good spots to hide from predators.

In cooler weather, rattlesnakes stay in dens with other snakes. A den can have hundreds of snakes in it.

Rattlesnakes may leave their den on sunny winter days. Lying in the sun warms their bodies.

FACT!

There may be different types of snakes in the same den.

The snakes often form a big ball to stay warm together all winter. They come out in the spring. The rattlesnakes return to the same den the next fall.

Chapter 5

RACCOONS

FACT FILE

ANIMAL GROUP: Mammal

DIET: Omnivore

HABITATS: Backyards, near ponds and streams, public spaces, urban areas, woodlands

Raccoons are known for their mask-like faces! They have black rings around their eyes and a long tail. They also have long toes with sharp claws. Their claws are good for climbing and cleaning out old dens. Raccoons will make their dens in rock piles, hollow logs, and holes in trees. They also use old dens and burrows left by other animals.

A mother raccoon usually has three or four babies, called kits. The kits stay in the den until they are two months old. After that, they follow their mother outside the den to look for food.

Camouflage helps protect this raccoon family outside their den.

FACT!

Just like people use bathrooms, raccoons will create a spot to poop. These areas are away from their dens.

The mother and kits share a den for about a year. Raccoons do not **hibernate** in winter. However, they can spend weeks in their dens without eating.

MORE ANIMAL DENS

BLACK BEARS

Black bears will make dens wherever they can find shelter. This may be in a cave or under some fallen trees. It may be inside a large, hollowed-out log. Black bears are the smallest bears in North America. They usually live in mountain forests or along the coasts.

LIONS

A lioness, or female lion, finds a den when it is time to give birth. She will use a hidden shelter, such as a cave. Lionesses hide their cubs inside the den to protect them. The cubs are born blind. They need their mother to give them food. She moves the cubs every few days to keep them safe. The cubs stay in the dens until they are two months old.

COYOTES

Coyotes like to make their dens under trees and rock piles. They may also use another animal's old den. Coyotes make more than one den entrance. Their entrances are often shaped like triangles.

SKUNKS

Skunks make their dens inside logs and rock piles. They will also make dens under walls, crawl spaces, and buildings. Skunks are about the size of a pet cat.

DEN DISCOVERY!

There are so many animals that live in dens! Bobcats, polar bears, opossums, rattlesnakes, and raccoons are some of them. Animals make dens to stay warm. They give birth in dens. They use dens to protect themselves and their babies. You might spot a den in your backyard or a park. Be careful, and do not get too close. This will help keep dens safe. You can also learn even more about animals that live in dens!

GLOSSARY

burrow (BUR-oh) a tunnel or hole in the ground made or used as a home by an animal

camouflage (KAM-uh-flahzh) to disguise something so that it blends in with its surroundings

carnivore (KAHR-nuh-vor) an animal that eats meat

cold-blooded (KOHLD-bluhd-id) having a body temperature that changes according to the temperature of the surroundings, like reptiles or fish

habitat (HAB-i-tat) the place where an animal or a plant is usually found

hibernate (HYE-bur-nate) when animals sleep for the entire winter; this protects them and helps them survive when the temperatures are cold and food is hard to find

mammal (MAM-uhl) a warm-blooded animal that has fur and usually gives birth to live babies

marsupial (mahr-SOO-pee-uhl) any of a large group of animals that includes kangaroos, koalas, and opossums; female marsupials carry their babies in pouches

nocturnal (nahk-TUR-nuhl) active at night

omnivore (AHM-nuh-vor) an animal that eats both plants and meat

predator (PRED-uh-tur) an animal that lives by hunting other animals for food

reptile (REP-tile) a cold-blooded animal that crawls across the ground or creeps on short legs; most reptiles have backbones and reproduce by laying eggs

INDEX

Page numbers in **bold** indicate images.

ABOUT THE AUTHOR

Claire Caprioli loves learning about animals and writing books for kids. Opossums, skunks, raccoons, and coyotes live in the woods by her home. One time a black bear walked through her backyard! You can learn more about her by visiting clairecaprioli.com.